FRENCH
COUNTRY
DIARY

Linda Dannenberg, Pierre
Moulin & Guy Bouchet

2 · 0 · 0 · 0

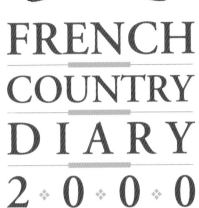

FRENCH
COUNTRY
DIARY
2·0·0·0

LINDA DANNENBERG
PIERRE MOULIN

PHOTOGRAPHY BY
GUY BOUCHET

POTTER
&
WORKMAN

CALENDARS

WORKMAN PUBLISHING
NEW YORK

*Calendars and diaries are available at special discounts when
purchased in bulk for premiums and sales promotions as well as
for fund-raising or educational use. Special editions can also be
created to specification. For details, contact the Special Sales
Director at the address below.*

Workman Publishing Company
708 Broadway
New York, New York 10003-9555

Printed in Italy

First printing August 1999

ISBN 0-7611-1521-8

*E*leven years ago, in our inaugural *French Country Diary,* we featured a region of France that epitomized the best of French country style and *art de vivre*—the beautiful and beguiling province of Provence. It is a land of gorgeous exaggeration—intense, luminous sunlight; impossibly rich and vivid colors; air heady with the fragrances of lavender, rosemary, and wild thyme; a relentless wind, the mistral, that sweeps the sky to a dazzling clarity; and multihued landscapes of such grace and harmony you would swear they are Van Gogh canvases come to life. To celebrate our entry into a new millennium, we have chosen to return to Provence for this year's *French Country Diary,* to extol a region with a character and style so unique and a *joie de vivre* so contagious that it stands alone, a principality in spirit if not in fact.

We visit quaint medieval villages lodged in the alpine foothills; patrician estates perched above the Mediterranean; pristine, sunwashed inns with lush lavender gardens; rustic kitchens of wood, tile, and stone; chic resort towns such as Saint-Tropez and Bandol; terrace tables laden with succulent Provençal fare; antique shops stocked with rare quilts, armoires, and vintage hats; and a private Riviera beach of powdery sand dotted with red, white, and blue parasols. In this year of years, we offer you 52 luminous, lovely weeks of discovery in this province closest to our hearts, and we wish you a joyful *Bonne Année*!

27
MONDAY

31
FRIDAY

28
TUESDAY

1
SATURDAY
New Year's Day

29
WEDNESDAY

2
SUNDAY

30
THURSDAY

NOTES:

▸ *Steep alpine cliffs form a protective backdrop for the flower-decked medieval village of Moustiers-Sainte-Marie.*

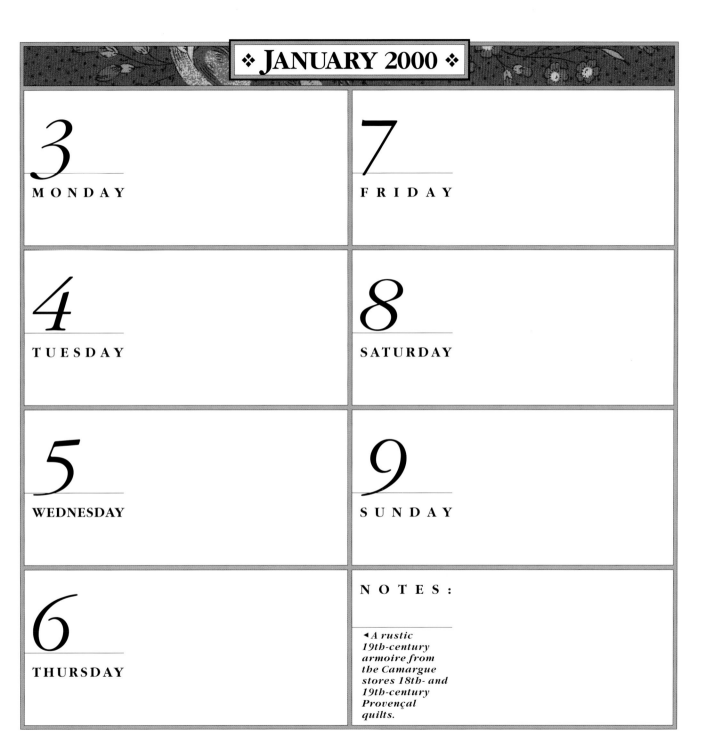

❖ JANUARY 2000 ❖

3
MONDAY

4
TUESDAY

5
WEDNESDAY

6
THURSDAY

7
FRIDAY

8
SATURDAY

9
SUNDAY

NOTES:

◄ A rustic 19th-century armoire from the Camargue stores 18th- and 19th-century Provençal quilts.

10
M O N D A Y

14
F R I D A Y

11
T U E S D A Y

15
S A T U R D A Y
Martin Luther King Jr.'s Birthday

12
WEDNESDAY

16
S U N D A Y

13
THURSDAY

N O T E S :

▶ *Young vines assert pride of place across the antique stone façade of a wine-producing estate in Le Beausset.*

❖ JANUARY 2000 ❖

17
MONDAY
Martin Luther King Day

18
TUESDAY

19
WEDNESDAY

20
THURSDAY

21
FRIDAY

22
SATURDAY

23
SUNDAY

NOTES:

▸ *Graceful clusters of lavender dominate the back garden of the Bastide de Capelongue, a new inn near Bonnieux.*

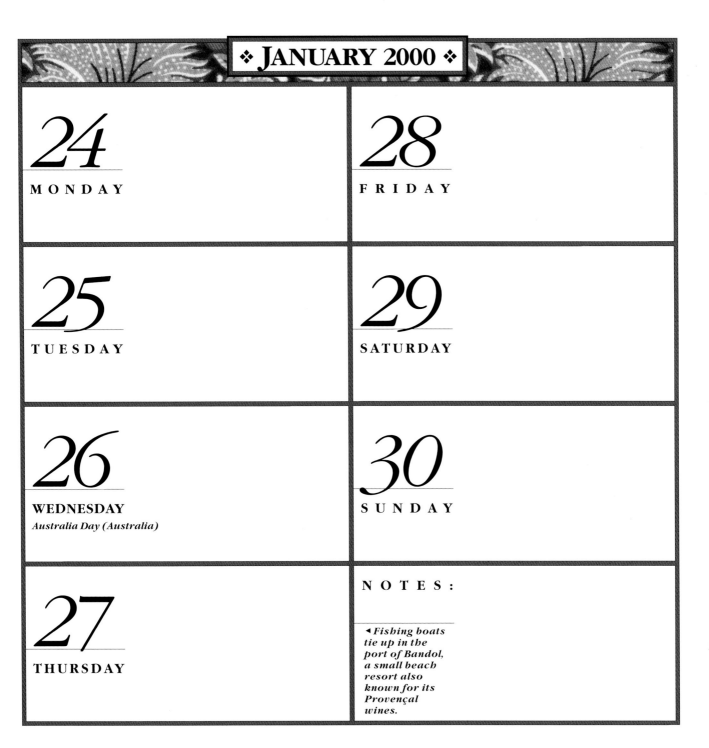

❖ JANUARY 2000 ❖

24
MONDAY

25
TUESDAY

26
WEDNESDAY
Australia Day (Australia)

27
THURSDAY

28
FRIDAY

29
SATURDAY

30
SUNDAY

NOTES:

◄ *Fishing boats tie up in the port of Bandol, a small beach resort also known for its Provençal wines.*

31
M O N D A Y

1
T U E S D A Y

2
WEDNESDAY

3
T H U R S D A Y

4
F R I D A Y

5
SATURDAY

6
S U N D A Y
Waitangi Day (New Zealand)

N O T E S :

◄ Façades washed with pink daub and colorful doorways characterize the little village of Villecroze.

❖ FEBRUARY 2000 ❖

7
M O N D A Y

11
F R I D A Y

8
T U E S D A Y

12
S A T U R D A Y
Lincoln's Birthday

9
W E D N E S D A Y

13
S U N D A Y

10
T H U R S D A Y

N O T E S :

▶ *In the Riviera hill town of Cotignac, the 16th-century houses have virtually disappeared behind greenery.*

❖ FEBRUARY 2000 ❖

14
M O N D A Y
Valentine's Day

15
T U E S D A Y

16
WEDNESDAY

17
T H U R S D A Y

18
F R I D A Y

19
S A T U R D A Y

20
S U N D A Y

N O T E S :

▸ *An antique stone heart and a venerable date adorn the door-way of a small village house in Le Castellet.*

21
MONDAY
Presidents Day

22
TUESDAY
Washington's Birthday

23
WEDNESDAY

24
THURSDAY

25
FRIDAY

26
SATURDAY

27
SUNDAY

NOTES:

▸ *A rustic cheese board offering two mild chêvre cheeses is set out for Sunday breakfast at a Lubéron home.*

28
MONDAY

29
TUESDAY

1
WEDNESDAY

2
THURSDAY

3
FRIDAY

4
SATURDAY

5
SUNDAY

NOTES:

◄ *At a quaint shop in La Palud-sur-Verdon, an old beaded screen lets breezes in and keeps flies out.*

6
MONDAY
Labor Day (WA, Australia)

7
TUESDAY

8
WEDNESDAY
Ash Wednesday

9
THURSDAY

10
FRIDAY

11
SATURDAY

12
SUNDAY

N O T E S :

▶ *At the end of the day, locals gather on the café terraces that dot the cobbled streets of Lourmarin.*

13
M O N D A Y
Labour Day (VIC, Australia)

14
T U E S D A Y

15
WEDNESDAY

16
THURSDAY

17
F R I D A Y
St. Patrick's Day

18
SATURDAY

19
S U N D A Y

N O T E S :

◄ *Near Bonnieux,
a wrought-iron
gate separates
a private garden
from vast fields
of lavender.*

❖ MARCH 2000 ❖

20
MONDAY

21
TUESDAY

22
WEDNESDAY

23
THURSDAY

24
FRIDAY

25
SATURDAY

26
SUNDAY

NOTES:

▸ *Provençal chef René Bérard teaches cooking classes in this rustic 17th-century kitchen in La Cadière d'Azur.*

27
M O N D A Y

31
F R I D A Y

28
T U E S D A Y

1
S A T U R D A Y

29
W E D N E S D A Y

2
S U N D A Y

30
T H U R S D A Y

N O T E S :

◄*Kayakers ply the gentle turquoise waters of the dramatic Gorges du Verdon.*

3
M O N D A Y

7
F R I D A Y

4
T U E S D A Y

8
S A T U R D A Y

5
WEDNESDAY

9
S U N D A Y

6
T H U R S D A Y

N O T E S :

◄ *High in the hills of Moustiers-Sainte-Marie, the bells of a Romanesque tower ring out the hour.*

❖ **APRIL 2000** ❖

10
MONDAY

11
TUESDAY

12
WEDNESDAY

13
THURSDAY

14
FRIDAY

15
SATURDAY

16
SUNDAY
Palm Sunday

NOTES:

► *At the Auberge de Lourmarin, chef Edward Loubet offers an irresistable trio of flavored crèmes brulées.*

17
MONDAY

18
TUESDAY

19
WEDNESDAY

20
THURSDAY
Passover

21
FRIDAY
Good Friday

22
SATURDAY

23
SUNDAY
Easter

NOTES:

▶ *In Isle-sur-Sorgue, an antiques dealer embellishes a banquette with a Provençal quilt and hat.*

❖ APRIL 2000 ❖

24
MONDAY

25
TUESDAY

Anzac Day
(Australia & New Zealand)

26
WEDNESDAY

27
THURSDAY

28
FRIDAY

29
SATURDAY

30
SUNDAY

NOTES:

▸ *A lush new growth of pale green leaves enrobes old, gnarled grapevines near Buis-les-Baronnies.*

1
MONDAY

*Labour Day
(QLD, Australia)*

2
TUESDAY

3
WEDNESDAY

4
THURSDAY

5
FRIDAY

6
SATURDAY

7
SUNDAY

NOTES:

◄ *The lovely,
artisanal beauty
products of
Côte Bastide
lend an air of
temps perdu to
a dressing table.*

8
MONDAY

9
TUESDAY

10
WEDNESDAY

11
THURSDAY

12
FRIDAY

13
SATURDAY

14
SUNDAY
Mother's Day

NOTES:

◄ The lively old fishing port of Marseilles bustles with fishing boats, sidewalk strollers and sun-washed cafés.

❖ MAY 2000 ❖

15
MONDAY

16
TUESDAY

17
WEDNESDAY

18
THURSDAY

19
FRIDAY

20
SATURDAY

21
SUNDAY

NOTES:

► *At the Bastide de Moustiers, chef Benoît Witz serves a refreshing chilled melon soup with fresh strawberries.*

❖ MAY 2000 ❖

22
MONDAY
Victoria Day (Canada)

23
TUESDAY

24
WEDNESDAY

25
THURSDAY

26
FRIDAY

27
SATURDAY

28
SUNDAY

NOTES:

◄ *An old watch-tower, topped by a terra-cotta tile roof, has been converted to a lovely vacation home in Trigance.*

❖ **MAY-JUNE 2000** ❖

29
M O N D A Y
Memorial Day Observed
Spring Bank Holiday (U.K.)

30
T U E S D A Y
Traditional Memorial Day

31
WEDNESDAY

1
THURSDAY

2
F R I D A Y

3
SATURDAY

4
S U N D A Y

N O T E S :

▸ *Glowing faïence, set atop an intricately stitched quilt, adorns a table at the Hostellerie Bérard.*

5
MONDAY

6
TUESDAY

7
WEDNESDAY

8
THURSDAY

9
FRIDAY

10
SATURDAY

11
SUNDAY

NOTES:

▶ *On a wine and olive-oil estate in Le Beausset, lavender and old olive trees form a magical landscape.*

12
MONDAY

16
FRIDAY

13
TUESDAY

17
SATURDAY

14
WEDNESDAY

18
SUNDAY
Father's Day

15
THURSDAY

NOTES:

◄ *A pastiche of bold colors and diverse architectural styles enlivens the small villages that dot the Côte d'Azur.*

19
M O N D A Y

20
T U E S D A Y

21
WEDNESDAY

22
THURSDAY

23
F R I D A Y

24
SATURDAY
St. Jean Baptiste Day
(Canada)

25
S U N D A Y

N O T E S :

▸ *Baskets of*
fresh herbs and
salad greens
are gathered
daily from chef
Alain Ducasse's
vast potager
in Moustiers.

Eruca sativa
Roquette

26
MONDAY

30
FRIDAY

27
TUESDAY

1
SATURDAY
Canada Day (Canada)

28
WEDNESDAY

2
SUNDAY

29
THURSDAY

NOTES:

◄ *A palette of whites and beiges enhances the architectural detailing in a dining room of the Bastide de Capelongue.*

3
MONDAY

4
TUESDAY
Independence Day

5
WEDNESDAY

6
THURSDAY

7
FRIDAY

8
SATURDAY

9
SUNDAY

NOTES:

◄ On a private beach in the fashionable Riviera resort of Sainte-Maxime, parasols provide welcome shade.

❖ JULY 2000 ❖

10
MONDAY

11
TUESDAY

12
WEDNESDAY

13
THURSDAY

14
FRIDAY

15
SATURDAY

16
SUNDAY

NOTES:

▸ *In the village of Saint-Pierre-de-Tourtour, climbing roses adorn the town hall.*

17
MONDAY

21
FRIDAY

18
TUESDAY

22
SATURDAY

19
WEDNESDAY

23
SUNDAY

20
THURSDAY

NOTES:

▸ *Soft-hued fabrics and an inviting antique canape welcome guests at Avignon's La Mirande.*

❖ JULY 2000 ❖

24
MONDAY

28
FRIDAY

25
TUESDAY

29
SATURDAY

26
WEDNESDAY

30
SUNDAY

27
THURSDAY

NOTES:

◄ *Vast fields of sunflowers— such as these along the road to Saint-Rémy— blanket much of Provence.*

31
MONDAY

4
FRIDAY

1
TUESDAY

5
SATURDAY

2
WEDNESDAY

6
SUNDAY

3
THURSDAY

NOTES:

▶ *The triple-tiered canal-tiled roof called a genoise characterizes many classic Provençal homes.*

7
MONDAY
Civic Holiday (Canada)
Summer Bank Holiday (Scotland)

8
TUESDAY

9
WEDNESDAY

10
THURSDAY

11
FRIDAY

12
SATURDAY

13
SUNDAY

NOTES:

◄ *From the cool, shady terrace of the Bastide de Moustiers, diners gaze out on fields of lavender and almond trees.*

14
MONDAY

15
TUESDAY

16
WEDNESDAY

17
THURSDAY

18
FRIDAY

19
SATURDAY

20
SUNDAY

N O T E S :

▸ *From its perch atop a gentle hill, a stone church dating from the 11th century crowns the small village of Tourtour.*

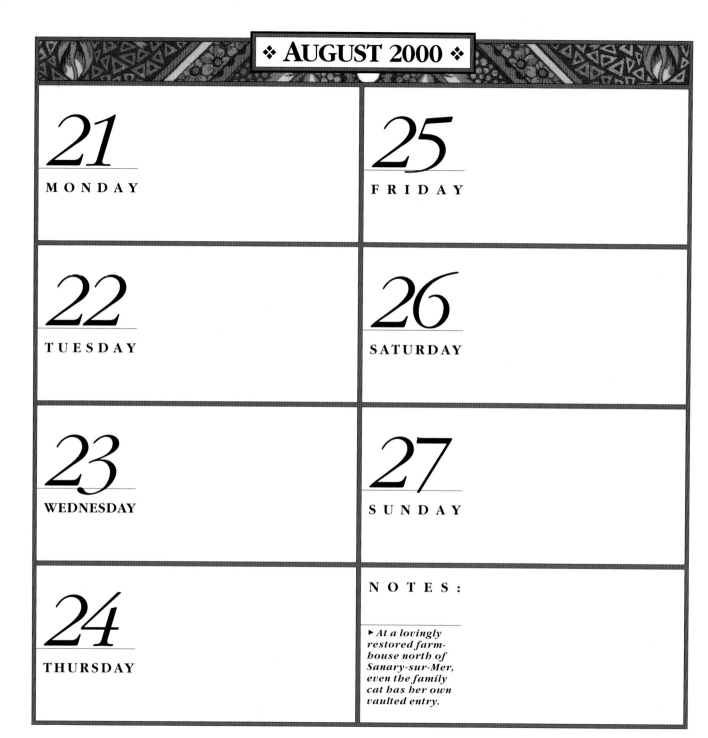

❖ **AUGUST 2000** ❖

21
MONDAY

22
TUESDAY

23
WEDNESDAY

24
THURSDAY

25
FRIDAY

26
SATURDAY

27
SUNDAY

NOTES:

► *At a lovingly restored farmhouse north of Sanary-sur-Mer, even the family cat has her own vaulted entry.*

28
MONDAY

Summer Bank Holiday
(England, Wales & N. Ireland)

29
TUESDAY

30
WEDNESDAY

31
THURSDAY

1
FRIDAY

2
SATURDAY

3
SUNDAY

NOTES:

◄ *Washed by the sun and whipped by the mistral, the Lubéron's terraced farms form a mottled patchwork.*

4
MONDAY
Labor Day

5
TUESDAY

6
WEDNESDAY

7
THURSDAY

8
FRIDAY

9
SATURDAY

10
SUNDAY
Grandparents Day

NOTES:

▶ *Portals in the ancient fortified walls of Le Castellet reveal glorious panoramas of the Mediterranean.*

11
MONDAY

15
FRIDAY

12
TUESDAY

16
SATURDAY

13
WEDNESDAY

17
SUNDAY

14
THURSDAY

NOTES:

◄ In the harbor of Saint-Tropez, a vintage wooden sloop ties up at one of the old stone quays.

18
MONDAY

19
TUESDAY

20
WEDNESDAY

21
THURSDAY

22
FRIDAY

23
SATURDAY

24
SUNDAY

NOTES:

▸ *Potted hydrangeas and a gurgling tiered fountain bring refreshing color and sound to a walled courtyard.*

25
MONDAY

26
TUESDAY

27
WEDNESDAY

28
THURSDAY

29
FRIDAY

30
SATURDAY
Rosh Hashanah

1
SUNDAY

NOTES:

▸ *An antique cart is laden with bounty from a morning's shopping trip to the market in Riez.*

2
MONDAY

Labour Day
(ACT, NSW & SA, Australia)

3
TUESDAY

4
WEDNESDAY

5
THURSDAY

6
FRIDAY

7
SATURDAY

8
SUNDAY

N O T E S :

◄ A thick vine canopy shades the garden table outside this 17th-century farmhouse near La Cadière d'Azur.

❖ OCTOBER 2000 ❖

9
MONDAY

Columbus Day Observed
Thanksgiving (Canada)
Yom Kippur

10
TUESDAY

11
WEDNESDAY

12
THURSDAY

Traditional Columbus Day

13
FRIDAY

14
SATURDAY

15
SUNDAY

NOTES:

▸ *A morning's harvest from the Bandol yields artichokes and a bouquet of flowering herbs.*

16
MONDAY

17
TUESDAY

18
WEDNESDAY

19
THURSDAY

20
FRIDAY

21
SATURDAY

22
SUNDAY

NOTES:

◄ *In the hill village of Trigance, an enamel-tiled bell tower seems inspired by Mediterranean colors.*

23
MONDAY
Labour Day (New Zealand)

24
TUESDAY

25
WEDNESDAY

26
THURSDAY

27
FRIDAY

28
SATURDAY

29
SUNDAY

NOTES:

► *Hundreds of subtle hues go into the décor of the white-glazed faïence produced at Atelier du Soleil.*

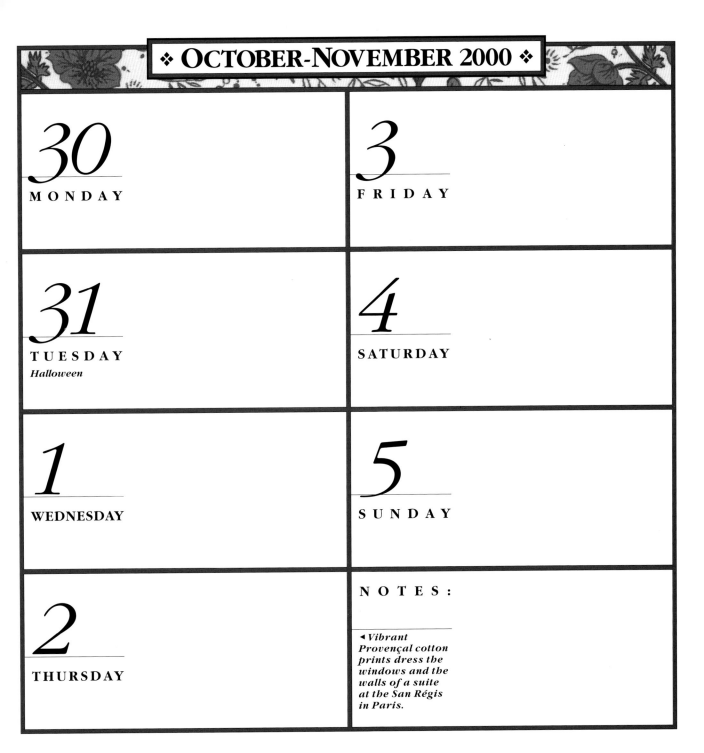

30
MONDAY

31
TUESDAY
Halloween

1
WEDNESDAY

2
THURSDAY

3
FRIDAY

4
SATURDAY

5
SUNDAY

NOTES:

◄Vibrant Provençal cotton prints dress the windows and the walls of a suite at the San Régis in Paris.

6
MONDAY

10
FRIDAY

7
TUESDAY
Election Day

11
SATURDAY
Veterans Day
Remembrance Day (Canada)

8
WEDNESDAY

12
SUNDAY

9
THURSDAY

NOTES:

▸ *Designed to look like a quaint fishing village, Port Grimaud is a modern Riviera resort threaded with canals.*

13
M O N D A Y

14
T U E S D A Y

15
WEDNESDAY

16
THURSDAY

17
F R I D A Y

18
SATURDAY

19
S U N D A Y

N O T E S :

◄ *Huge oak casks age several vintages of wines at the Domaine de Souviou in Le Beausset.*

20
MONDAY

21
TUESDAY

22
WEDNESDAY

23
THURSDAY
Thanksgiving

24
FRIDAY

25
SATURDAY

26
SUNDAY

NOTES:

▶ *Rustic wood cabinetry and an antique harvest table add warmth to a restored kitchen near La Cadière d'Azur.*

27
MONDAY

1
FRIDAY

28
TUESDAY

2
SATURDAY

29
WEDNESDAY

3
SUNDAY

30
THURSDAY

NOTES:

◄ *The garden of the Mas des Graviers, a B&B in the village of Pourrières, is still vibrant in winter.*

4
MONDAY

5
TUESDAY

6
WEDNESDAY

7
THURSDAY

8
FRIDAY

9
SATURDAY

10
SUNDAY

N O T E S :

▸ *In a small square behind the harbor in Saint-Tropez, cafés close up shop at the end of a balmy afternoon.*

11
MONDAY

12
TUESDAY

13
WEDNESDAY

14
THURSDAY

15
FRIDAY

16
SATURDAY

17
SUNDAY

NOTES:

▶ *Chef Edouard Loubet prepares an elegant fruit dessert crowned by caramelized sugar.*

18
MONDAY

19
TUESDAY

20
WEDNESDAY

21
THURSDAY

22
FRIDAY
Hanukkah

23
SATURDAY

24
SUNDAY

N O T E S :

◄ The markets of Old Nice offer bright marzipan "vegetables" and "fruits" for the Christmas table.

❖ DECEMBER 2000 ❖

25
MONDAY
Christmas

26
TUESDAY
Boxing Day

27
WEDNESDAY

28
THURSDAY

29
FRIDAY

30
SATURDAY

31
SUNDAY

NOTES:

▸ *Lavish, elegant desserts are a hallmark of a visit to the Chateau du Domaine Saint-Martin, near Vence.*

❖ 2 0 0 0 ❖

JANUARY

S	M	T	W	T	F	S
						1
2	3	4	5	6	7	8
9	10	11	12	13	14	15
16	17	18	19	20	21	22
23/30	24/31	25	26	27	28	29

FEBRUARY

S	M	T	W	T	F	S
		1	2	3	4	5
6	7	8	9	10	11	12
13	14	15	16	17	18	19
20	21	22	23	24	25	26
27	28	29				

MARCH

S	M	T	W	T	F	S
			1	2	3	4
5	6	7	8	9	10	11
12	13	14	15	16	17	18
19	20	21	22	23	24	25
26	27	28	29	30	31	

APRIL

S	M	T	W	T	F	S
						1
2	3	4	5	6	7	8
9	10	11	12	13	14	15
16	17	18	19	20	21	22
23/30	24	25	26	27	28	29

MAY

S	M	T	W	T	F	S
	1	2	3	4	5	6
7	8	9	10	11	12	13
14	15	16	17	18	19	20
21	22	23	24	25	26	27
28	29	30	31			

JUNE

S	M	T	W	T	F	S
				1	2	3
4	5	6	7	8	9	10
11	12	13	14	15	16	17
18	19	20	21	22	23	24
25	26	27	28	29	30	

JULY

S	M	T	W	T	F	S
						1
2	3	4	5	6	7	8
9	10	11	12	13	14	15
16	17	18	19	20	21	22
23/30	24/31	25	26	27	28	29

AUGUST

S	M	T	W	T	F	S
		1	2	3	4	5
6	7	8	9	10	11	12
13	14	15	16	17	18	19
20	21	22	23	24	25	26
27	28	29	30	31		

SEPTEMBER

S	M	T	W	T	F	S
					1	2
3	4	5	6	7	8	9
10	11	12	13	14	15	16
17	18	19	20	21	22	23
24	25	26	27	28	29	30

OCTOBER

S	M	T	W	T	F	S
1	2	3	4	5	6	7
8	9	10	11	12	13	14
15	16	17	18	19	20	21
22	23	24	25	26	27	28
29	30	31				

NOVEMBER

S	M	T	W	T	F	S
			1	2	3	4
5	6	7	8	9	10	11
12	13	14	15	16	17	18
19	20	21	22	23	24	25
26	27	28	29	30		

DECEMBER

S	M	T	W	T	F	S
					1	2
3	4	5	6	7	8	9
10	11	12	13	14	15	16
17	18	19	20	21	22	23
24/31	25	26	27	28	29	30

❖ 2 0 0 1 ❖

JANUARY

S	M	T	W	T	F	S
	1	2	3	4	5	6
7	8	9	10	11	12	13
14	15	16	17	18	19	20
21	22	23	24	25	26	27
28	29	30	31			

FEBRUARY

S	M	T	W	T	F	S
				1	2	3
4	5	6	7	8	9	10
11	12	13	14	15	16	17
18	19	20	21	22	23	24
25	26	27	28			

MARCH

S	M	T	W	T	F	S
				1	2	3
4	5	6	7	8	9	10
11	12	13	14	15	16	17
18	19	20	21	22	23	24
25	26	27	28	29	30	31

APRIL

S	M	T	W	T	F	S
1	2	3	4	5	6	7
8	9	10	11	12	13	14
15	16	17	18	19	20	21
22	23	24	25	26	27	28
29	30					

MAY

S	M	T	W	T	F	S
		1	2	3	4	5
6	7	8	9	10	11	12
13	14	15	16	17	18	19
20	21	22	23	24	25	26
27	28	29	30	31		

JUNE

S	M	T	W	T	F	S
					1	2
3	4	5	6	7	8	9
10	11	12	13	14	15	16
17	18	19	20	21	22	23
24	25	26	27	28	29	30

JULY

S	M	T	W	T	F	S
1	2	3	4	5	6	7
8	9	10	11	12	13	14
15	16	17	18	19	20	21
22	23	24	25	26	27	28
29	30	31				

AUGUST

S	M	T	W	T	F	S
			1	2	3	4
5	6	7	8	9	10	11
12	13	14	15	16	17	18
19	20	21	22	23	24	25
26	27	28	29	30	31	

SEPTEMBER

S	M	T	W	T	F	S
						1
2	3	4	5	6	7	8
9	10	11	12	13	14	15
16	17	18	19	20	21	22
23/30	24	25	26	27	28	29

OCTOBER

S	M	T	W	T	F	S
	1	2	3	4	5	6
7	8	9	10	11	12	13
14	15	16	17	18	19	20
21	22	23	24	25	26	27
28	29	30	31			

NOVEMBER

S	M	T	W	T	F	S
				1	2	3
4	5	6	7	8	9	10
11	12	13	14	15	16	17
18	19	20	21	22	23	24
25	26	27	28	29	30	

DECEMBER

S	M	T	W	T	F	S
						1
2	3	4	5	6	7	8
9	10	11	12	13	14	15
16	17	18	19	20	21	22
23/30	24/31	25	26	27	28	29

❖ A • B ❖

N A M E

ADDRESS

P H O N E

N A M E

ADDRESS

P H O N E

N A M E

ADDRESS

P H O N E

N A M E

ADDRESS

P H O N E

N A M E

ADDRESS

P H O N E

N A M E

ADDRESS

P H O N E

N A M E

ADDRESS

P H O N E

N A M E

ADDRESS

P H O N E

N A M E

ADDRESS

P H O N E

N A M E

ADDRESS

P H O N E

N A M E

ADDRESS

P H O N E

N A M E

ADDRESS

P H O N E

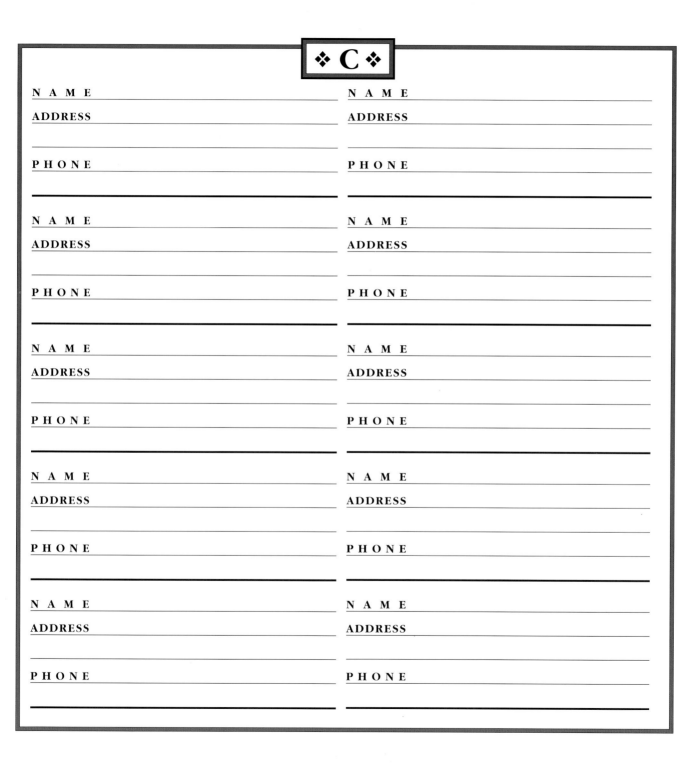

❖ C ❖

NAME

ADDRESS

PHONE

NAME

ADDRESS

PHONE

NAME

ADDRESS

PHONE

NAME

ADDRESS

PHONE

NAME

ADDRESS

PHONE

NAME

ADDRESS

PHONE

NAME

ADDRESS

PHONE

NAME

ADDRESS

PHONE

NAME

ADDRESS

PHONE

NAME

ADDRESS

PHONE

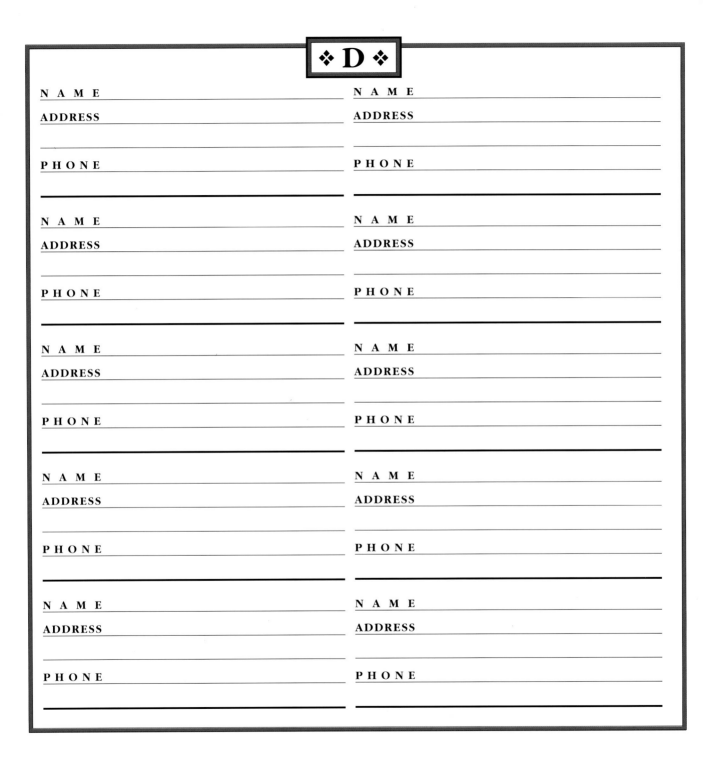

❖ D ❖

NAME

ADDRESS

PHONE

NAME

ADDRESS

PHONE

NAME

ADDRESS

PHONE

NAME

ADDRESS

PHONE

NAME

ADDRESS

PHONE

NAME

ADDRESS

PHONE

NAME

ADDRESS

PHONE

NAME

ADDRESS

PHONE

NAME

ADDRESS

PHONE

NAME

ADDRESS

PHONE

❖ E • F ❖

NAME

ADDRESS

PHONE

NAME

ADDRESS

PHONE

NAME

ADDRESS

PHONE

NAME

ADDRESS

PHONE

NAME

ADDRESS

PHONE

NAME

ADDRESS

PHONE

NAME

ADDRESS

PHONE

NAME

ADDRESS

PHONE

NAME

ADDRESS

PHONE

NAME

ADDRESS

PHONE

G

NAME	NAME
ADDRESS	ADDRESS
PHONE	PHONE

NAME	NAME
ADDRESS	ADDRESS
PHONE	PHONE

NAME	NAME
ADDRESS	ADDRESS
PHONE	PHONE

NAME	NAME
ADDRESS	ADDRESS
PHONE	PHONE

NAME	NAME
ADDRESS	ADDRESS
PHONE	PHONE

❖ H • I ❖

NAME

ADDRESS

PHONE

NAME

ADDRESS

PHONE

NAME

ADDRESS

PHONE

NAME

ADDRESS

PHONE

NAME

ADDRESS

PHONE

NAME

ADDRESS

PHONE

NAME

ADDRESS

PHONE

NAME

ADDRESS

PHONE

NAME

ADDRESS

PHONE

NAME

ADDRESS

PHONE

❖ J · K ❖

NAME

ADDRESS

PHONE

NAME

ADDRESS

PHONE

NAME

ADDRESS

PHONE

NAME

ADDRESS

PHONE

NAME

ADDRESS

PHONE

NAME

ADDRESS

PHONE

NAME

ADDRESS

PHONE

NAME

ADDRESS

PHONE

NAME

ADDRESS

PHONE

NAME

ADDRESS

PHONE

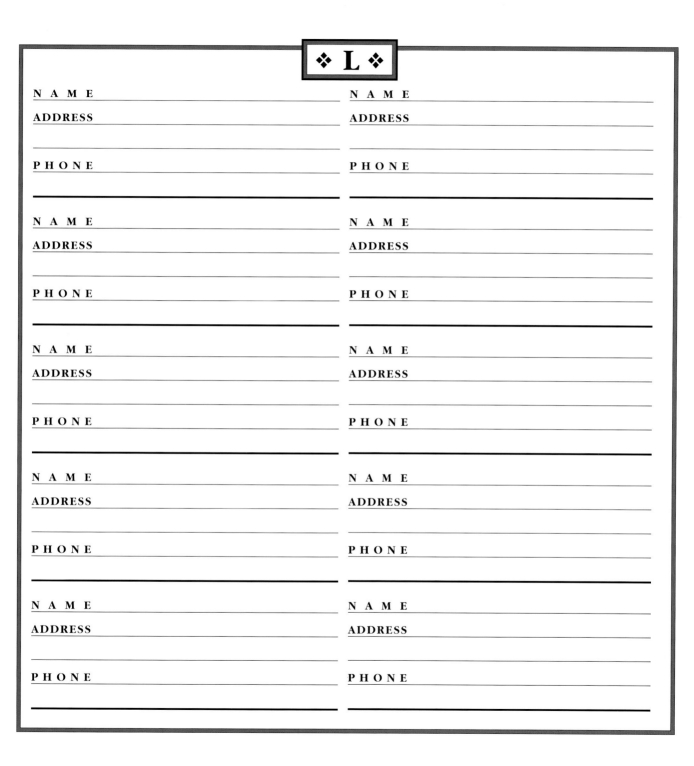

❖ **L** ❖

NAME

ADDRESS

PHONE

NAME

ADDRESS

PHONE

NAME

ADDRESS

PHONE

NAME

ADDRESS

PHONE

NAME

ADDRESS

PHONE

NAME

ADDRESS

PHONE

NAME

ADDRESS

PHONE

NAME

ADDRESS

PHONE

NAME

ADDRESS

PHONE

NAME

ADDRESS

PHONE

❖ M • N ❖

NAME

ADDRESS

PHONE

NAME

ADDRESS

PHONE

NAME

ADDRESS

PHONE

NAME

ADDRESS

PHONE

NAME

ADDRESS

PHONE

NAME

ADDRESS

PHONE

NAME

ADDRESS

PHONE

NAME

ADDRESS

PHONE

NAME

ADDRESS

PHONE

NAME

ADDRESS

PHONE

❖ O • P ❖

NAME

ADDRESS

PHONE

NAME

ADDRESS

PHONE

NAME

ADDRESS

PHONE

NAME

ADDRESS

PHONE

NAME

ADDRESS

PHONE

NAME

ADDRESS

PHONE

NAME

ADDRESS

PHONE

NAME

ADDRESS

PHONE

NAME

ADDRESS

PHONE

NAME

ADDRESS

PHONE

❖ Q · R ❖

N A M E

ADDRESS

PHONE

N A M E

ADDRESS

PHONE

N A M E

ADDRESS

PHONE

N A M E

ADDRESS

PHONE

N A M E

ADDRESS

PHONE

N A M E

ADDRESS

PHONE

N A M E

ADDRESS

PHONE

N A M E

ADDRESS

PHONE

N A M E

ADDRESS

PHONE

N A M E

ADDRESS

PHONE

S

N A M E

ADDRESS

P H O N E

N A M E

ADDRESS

P H O N E

N A M E

ADDRESS

P H O N E

N A M E

ADDRESS

P H O N E

N A M E

ADDRESS

P H O N E

N A M E

ADDRESS

P H O N E

N A M E

ADDRESS

P H O N E

N A M E

ADDRESS

P H O N E

N A M E

ADDRESS

P H O N E

N A M E

ADDRESS

P H O N E

❖ T ❖

NAME

ADDRESS

PHONE

NAME

ADDRESS

PHONE

NAME

ADDRESS

PHONE

NAME

ADDRESS

PHONE

NAME

ADDRESS

PHONE

NAME

ADDRESS

PHONE

NAME

ADDRESS

PHONE

NAME

ADDRESS

PHONE

NAME

ADDRESS

PHONE

NAME

ADDRESS

PHONE

❖ U · V · W ❖

NAME

ADDRESS

PHONE

NAME

ADDRESS

PHONE

NAME

ADDRESS

PHONE

NAME

ADDRESS

PHONE

NAME

ADDRESS

PHONE

NAME

ADDRESS

PHONE

NAME

ADDRESS

PHONE

NAME

ADDRESS

PHONE

NAME

ADDRESS

PHONE

NAME

ADDRESS

PHONE

❖ X · Y · Z ❖

NAME

ADDRESS

PHONE

NAME

ADDRESS

PHONE

NAME

ADDRESS

PHONE

NAME

ADDRESS

PHONE

NAME

ADDRESS

PHONE

NAME

ADDRESS

PHONE

NAME

ADDRESS

PHONE

NAME

ADDRESS

PHONE

NAME

ADDRESS

PHONE

NAME

ADDRESS

PHONE